AGRICULTURAL LABOR RELATIONS ACT
LABOR CODE SECTION 1140-1166.3
As Amended Effective January 1, 2012

1140. This part shall be known and may be referred to as the Alatorre-Zenovich-Dunlap-Berman Agricultural Labor Relations Act of 1975.

1140.2. It is hereby stated to be the policy of the State of California to encourage and protect the right of agricultural employees to full freedom of association, self-organization, and designation of representatives of their own choosing, to negotiate the terms and conditions of their employment, and to be free from the interference, restraint, or coercion of employers of labor, or their agents, in the designation of such representatives or in self-organization or in other concerted activities for the purpose of collective bargaining or other mutual aid or protection. For this purpose this part is adopted to provide for collective-bargaining rights for agricultural employees.

1140.4. As used in this part:
   (a) The term "agriculture" includes farming in all its branches, and, among other things, includes the cultivation and tillage of the soil, dairying, the production, cultivation, growing, and harvesting of any agricultural or horticultural commodities (including commodities defined as agricultural commodities in Section 1141j(g) of Title 12 of the United States Code), the raising of livestock, bees, furbearing animals, or poultry, and any practices (including any forestry or lumbering operations) performed by a farmer or on a farm as an incident to or in conjunction with such farming operations, including preparation for market and delivery to storage or to market or to carriers for transportation to market.
   (b) The term "agricultural employee" or "employee" shall mean one engaged in agriculture, as such term is defined in subdivision (a). However, nothing in this subdivision shall be construed to include any person other than those employees excluded from the coverage of the National Labor Relations Act, as amended, as agricultural employees, pursuant to Section 2(3) of the Labor Management Relations Act (Section 152(3), Title 29, United States Code), and Section 3(f) of the Fair Labor Standards Act (Section 203(f), Title 29, United States Code).
   Further, nothing in this part shall apply, or be construed to apply, to any employee who performs work to be done at the site of the construction, alteration, painting, or repair of a building, structure, or other work (as these terms have been construed under Section 8(e) of the Labor Management Relations Act, 29 U.S.C. Sec. 158(e)) or logging or timber-clearing operations in initial preparation of land for farming, or who does land leveling or only land surveying for any of the above.
   As used in this subdivision, "land leveling" shall include only major land moving operations changing the contour of the land, but shall not include annual or seasonal tillage or preparation of land

for cultivation.

(c) The term "agricultural employer" shall be liberally construed to include any person acting directly or indirectly in the interest of an employer in relation to an agricultural employee, any individual grower, corporate grower, cooperative grower, harvesting association, hiring association, land management group, any association of persons or cooperatives engaged in agriculture, and shall include any person who owns or leases or manages land used for agricultural purposes, but shall exclude any person supplying agricultural workers to an employer, any farm labor contractor as defined by Section 1682, and any person functioning in the capacity of a labor contractor. The employer engaging such labor contractor or person shall be deemed the employer for all purposes under this part.

(d) The term "person" shall mean one or more individuals, corporations, partnerships, limited liability companies, associations, legal representatives, trustees in bankruptcy, receivers, or any other legal entity, employer, or labor organization having an interest in the outcome of a proceeding under this part.

(e) The term "representatives" includes any individual or labor organization.

(f) The term "labor organization" means any organization of any kind, or any agency or employee representation committee or plan, in which employees participate and which exists, in whole or in part, for the purpose of dealing with employers concerning grievances, labor disputes, wages, rates of pay, hours of employment, or conditions of work for agricultural employees.

(g) The term "unfair labor practice" means any unfair labor practice specified in Chapter 4 (commencing with Section 1153) of this part.

(h) The term "labor dispute" includes any controversy concerning terms, tenure, or conditions of employment, or concerning the association or representation of persons in negotiating, fixing, maintaining, changing, or seeking to arrange terms or conditions of employment, regardless of whether the disputants stand in the proximate relation of employer and employee.

(i) The term "board" means Agricultural Labor Relations Board.

(j) The term "supervisor" means any individual having the authority, in the interest of the employer, to hire, transfer, suspend, lay off, recall, promote, discharge, assign, reward, or discipline other employees, or the responsibility to direct them, or to adjust their grievances, or effectively to recommend such action, if, in connection with the foregoing, the exercise of such authority is not of a merely routine or clerical nature, but requires the use of independent judgment.

1141. (a) There is hereby created in the Labor and Workforce Development Agency the Agricultural Labor Relations Board, which shall consist of five members.

(b) The members of the board shall be appointed by the Governor with the advice and consent of the Senate. The term of office of the members shall be five years, and the terms shall be staggered at one-year intervals. Upon the initial appointment, one member shall be appointed for a term ending January 1, 1977, one member shall be appointed for a term ending January 1, 1978, one member shall be appointed for a term ending January 1, 1979, one member shall be appointed for a term ending January 1, 1980, and one member shall be appointed for a term ending January 1, 1981. Any individual appointed to fill a vacancy of any member shall be appointed only for the unexpired term of the member to whose term he or she is succeeding. The Governor shall designate one member to serve as chairperson of the board. Any member of the board may be removed by the Governor, upon notice and hearing, for neglect of duty or malfeasance in office, but for no other cause.

1142. (a) The principal office of the board shall be in Sacramento, but it may meet and exercise any or all of its power at any other place in California.

(b) Besides the principal office in Sacramento, as provided in subdivision (a), the board may establish offices in such other cities as it shall deem necessary. The board may delegate to the personnel of these offices such powers as it deems appropriate to determine the unit appropriate for the purpose of collective bargaining, to investigate and provide for hearings, to determine whether a question of representation exists, to direct an election by a secret ballot pursuant to the provisions of Chapter 5 (commencing with Section 1156), and to certify the results of such election, and to investigate, conduct hearings and make determinations relating to unfair labor practices. The board may review any action taken pursuant to the authority delegated under this section upon a request for a review of such action filed with the board by an interested party. Any such review made by the board shall not, unless specifically ordered by the board, operate as a stay of any action taken. The entire record considered by the board in considering or acting upon any such request or review shall be made available to all parties prior to such consideration or action, and the board's findings and action thereon shall be published as a decision of the board.

1142.5. (a) The board shall maintain, at its principal office, a telephone line 24 hours a day, seven days a week, for the purpose of providing interested persons with information concerning their rights and responsibilities under this part, or for referring such persons to the appropriate agency or entity with the capacity to render advice or help in dealing with any situation arising out of agricultural labor disputes.

In order to carry out its responsibilities pursuant to this subdivision, the board may contract with an answering service to receive telephone messages during periods of time that its principal office is normally not open for business. Such messages shall be transmitted to the board on the board's next business day, or at such earlier time as the board specifies, or to its designated representative at the earliest possible time.

(b) Whenever a petition for an election has been filed in a bargaining unit in which a majority of the employees are engaged in a strike, the necessary and appropriate services of the board in the region in which the election will be held shall be available to the parties involved 24 hours a day until the election is held.

1143. The board shall, at the close of each fiscal year, make a report in writing to the Legislature and to the Governor stating in detail the cases it has heard, the decisions it has rendered, the names, salaries, and duties of all employees and officers in the employ or under the supervision of the board, and an account of all moneys it has disbursed.

1144. The board may from time to time make, amend, and rescind, in the manner prescribed in Chapter 3.5 (commencing with Section 11340) of Part 1 of Division 3 of Title 2 of the Government Code, such rules and regulations as may be necessary to carry out this part.

1144.5. (a) Notwithstanding Section 11425.10 of the Government Code, Chapter 4.5 (commencing with Section 11400) of Part 1 of Division 3 of Title 2 of the Government Code does not apply to a hearing by the board under this part, except a hearing to determine an unfair labor practice charge.

(b) Notwithstanding Sections 11425.30 and 11430.10 of the Government Code, in a hearing to determine an unfair labor practice charge, a person who has participated in a determination of probable cause, injunctive or other pre-hearing relief, or other equivalent preliminary determination in an adjudicative proceeding may serve as presiding officer or as a supervisor of the presiding officer or may assist or advise the presiding officer in the same proceeding.

1145. The board may appoint an executive secretary and such attorneys, hearing officers, administrative law officers, and other employees as it may from time to time find necessary for the proper performance of its duties. Attorneys appointed pursuant to this section may, at the discretion of the board, appear for and represent the board in any case in court. All employees appointed by the board shall perform their duties in an objective and impartial manner without prejudice toward any party subject to the jurisdiction of the board.

1146. The board is authorized to delegate to any group of three or more board members any or all the powers which it may itself exercise. A vacancy in the board shall not impair the right of the remaining members to exercise all the powers of the board, and three members shall at all times constitute a quorum. A vacancy shall be filled in the same manner as an original appointment.

1147. Each member of the board shall receive the salary provided for by Chapter 6 (commencing with Section 11550) of Part 1 of Division 3 of Title 2 of the Government Code.

1148. The board shall follow applicable precedents of the National Labor Relations Act, as amended.

1149. There shall be a general counsel of the board who shall be appointed by the Governor, subject to confirmation by a majority of the Senate, for a term of four years. The general counsel shall have the power to appoint such attorneys, administrative assistants, and other employees as necessary for the proper exercise of his duties. The general counsel of the board shall exercise general supervision over all attorneys employed by the board (other than administrative law officers and legal assistants to board members), and over the officers and employees in the regional offices. He shall have final authority, on behalf of the board, with respect to the investigation of charges and issuance of complaints under Chapter 6 (commencing with Section 1160) of this part, and with respect to the prosecution of such complaints before the board. He shall have such other duties as the board may prescribe or as may be provided by law. All employees appointed by the general counsel shall perform their duties in an objective and impartial manner without prejudice toward any party subject to the jurisdiction of the board. In case of a vacancy in the office of the general counsel, the Governor is authorized to designate the officer or employee who shall act as general counsel during such vacancy, but no person or persons so designated shall so act either (1) for more than 40 days when the Legislature is in session unless a nomination to fill such vacancy shall have been submitted to the Senate, or (2) after the adjournment sine die of the session of the Senate in which such nomination was submitted.

1150. Each member of the board and the general counsel of the board shall be eligible for reappointment, and shall not engage in any other business, vocation, or employment.

1151. For the purpose of all hearings and investigations, which, in the opinion of the board, are necessary and proper for the exercise of the powers vested in it by Chapters 5 (commencing with Section 1156) and 6 (commencing with Section 1160) of this part:
   (a) The board, or its duly authorized agents or agencies, shall at all reasonable times have access to, for the purpose of examination, and the right to copy, any evidence of any person being investigated or proceeded against that relates to any matter under investigation or in question. The members of the board or their designees or their duly authorized agents shall have the right of free access to all places of labor. The board, or any member thereof, shall upon application of any party to such proceedings, forthwith issue to such party subpoenas requiring the attendance and testimony of witnesses or the production of any evidence in such proceeding or investigation requested in such application. Within five days after the service of a subpoena on any person requiring the production of any evidence in his possession or under his control, such person may petition the board to revoke, and the board shall revoke, such subpoena if in its opinion the evidence whose production is required does not relate to any matter under investigation, or any matter in question in such proceedings, or if in its opinion such subpoena does not describe with sufficient particularity the evidence whose production is required. Any member of the board, or any agent or agency designated by the board for such purposes, may administer oaths and affirmations, examine witnesses, and receive evidence. Such attendance of witnesses and the production of such evidence may be

required from any place in the state at any designated place of hearing.

(b) In case of contumacy or refusal to obey a subpoena issued to any person, any superior court in any county within the jurisdiction of which the inquiry is carried on, or within the jurisdiction of which such person allegedly guilty of contumacy or refusal to obey is found or resides or transacts business, shall, upon application by the board, have jurisdiction to issue to such person an order requiring such person to appear before the board, its member, agent, or agency, there to produce evidence if so ordered, or there to give testimony touching the matter under investigation or in question. Any failure to obey such order of the court may be punished by such court as a contempt thereof.

1151.2. (a) No person shall be excused from attending and testifying, or from producing books, records, correspondence, documents, or other evidence in obedience to the subpoena of the board, on the ground that the testimony or evidence required of him may tend to incriminate him or subject him to a penalty or forfeiture. However, no individual shall be prosecuted or subjected to any penalty or forfeiture for or on account of any transaction, matter, or thing concerning which he is compelled, after having claimed his privilege against self-incrimination, to testify or produce evidence, except that such individual so testifying shall not be exempt from prosecution and punishment for perjury committed in so testifying.

(b) No individual shall be granted immunity pursuant to subdivision (a) unless, at least 10 calendar days prior thereto, the board has given written notice, by registered mail, to the district attorney of each county who may have reasonable grounds for objecting to such grant of immunity. Such notice shall specify the subject matter of the inquiries to which the witness' answers are to be immunized from use.

The board may not grant immunity in any case where it finds that a district attorney has reasonable grounds for objecting to such grant of immunity provided that the board may disregard objections that are not accompanied by the declaration of the district attorney that he or she is familiar with the notice and which sets forth the grounds for resisting such grant of immunity.

1151.3. Any party shall have the right to appear at any hearing in person, by counsel, or by other representative.

1151.4. (a) Complaints, orders, and other process and papers of the board, its members, agents, or agency, may be served either personally or by registered mail or by telegraph, or by leaving a copy thereof at the principal office or place of business of the person required to be served. The verified return by the individual so serving the same setting forth the manner of such service shall be proof of the same, and the return post office receipt or telegraph receipt therefor when registered and mailed or telegraphed as provided in this subdivision shall be proof of service of the same. Witnesses summoned before the board, its members, agents, or agency, shall be paid the same fees and mileage that are paid witnesses in the courts of the state, and witnesses whose depositions are taken and the persons taking the same shall severally be entitled to the same fees as are paid for like services in the courts of the state.

(b) All process of any court to which application may be made under this part may be served in the county where the defendant or other person required to be served resides or may be found.

1151.5. The several departments and agencies of the state upon request by the board, shall furnish the board all records, papers, and information in their possession, not otherwise privileged, relating to any matter before the board.

1151.6. Any person who shall willfully resist, prevent, impede, or interfere with any member of the board or any of its agents or agencies in the performance of duties pursuant to this part shall be guilty of a misdemeanor, and shall be punished by a fine of not more than five thousand ($5,000) dollars.

1152. Employees shall have the right to self-organization, to form, join, or assist labor organizations, to bargain collectively through representatives of their own choosing, and to engage in other concerted activities for the purpose of collective bargaining or other mutual aid or protection, and shall also have the right to refrain from any or all of such activities except to the extent that such right may be affected by an agreement requiring membership in a labor organization as a condition of continued employment as authorized in subdivision (c) of Section 1153.

1153. It shall be an unfair labor practice for an agricultural employer to do any of the following:

(a) To interfere with, restrain, or coerce agricultural employees in the exercise of the rights guaranteed in Section 1152.

(b) To dominate or interfere with the formation or administration of any labor organization or contribute financial or other support to it. However, subject to such rules and regulations as may be made and published by the board pursuant to Section 1144, an agricultural employer shall not be prohibited from permitting agricultural employees to confer with him during working hours without loss of time or pay.

(c) By discrimination in regard to the hiring or tenure of employment, or any term or condition of employment, to encourage or discourage membership in any labor organization.

Nothing in this part, or in any other statute of this state, shall preclude an agricultural employer from making an agreement with a labor organization (not established, maintained, or assisted by any action defined in this section as an unfair labor practice) to require as a condition of employment, membership therein on or after the fifth day following the beginning of such employment, or the effective date of such agreement whichever is later, if such labor organization is the representative of the agricultural employees as provided in Section 1156 in the appropriate collective-bargaining unit covered by such agreement. No employee who has been required to pay dues to a labor organization by virtue of his employment as an agricultural worker during any calendar month, shall be required to pay dues to another labor organization by virtue of similar employment during such month. For purposes of this chapter, membership shall mean the satisfaction of all reasonable terms and conditions uniformly applicable to other members in good standing; provided, that such membership shall not be denied or terminated except in compliance with a constitution or bylaws which afford full and fair rights to speech, assembly, and equal voting and membership privileges for all members, and which contain adequate procedures to assure due process to members and applicants for membership.

(d) To discharge or otherwise discriminate against an agricultural employee because he has filed charges or given testimony under this part.

(e) To refuse to bargain collectively in good faith with labor organizations certified pursuant to the provisions of Chapter 5 (commencing with Section 1156) of this part.

(f) To recognize, bargain with, or sign a collective-bargaining agreement with any labor organization not certified pursuant to the provisions of this part.

1154. It shall be an unfair labor practice for a labor organization or its agents to do any of the following:

(a) To restrain or coerce:

(1) Agricultural employees in the exercise of the rights guaranteed in Section 1152. This paragraph shall not impair the right of a labor organization to prescribe its own rules with respect to the acquisition or retention of membership therein.

(2) An agricultural employer in the selection of his representatives for the purposes of collective bargaining or the adjustment of grievances.

(b) To cause or attempt to cause an agricultural employer to discriminate against an employee in violation of subdivision (c) of Section 1153, or to discriminate against an employee with respect to whom membership in such organization has been denied or terminated for reasons other than failure to satisfy the membership requirements specified in subdivision (c) of Section 1153.

(c) To refuse to bargain collectively in good faith with an agricultural employer, provided it is the representative of his employees subject to the provisions of Chapter 5 (commencing with Section 1156) of this part.

(d) To do either of the following: (i) To engage in, or to induce or encourage any individual employed by any person to engage in, a strike or a refusal in the course of his employment to use, manufacture, process, transport, or otherwise handle or work on any goods, articles, materials, or commodities, or to perform any services; or (ii) to threaten, coerce, or restrain any person; where in either case (i) or (ii) an object thereof is any of the following:

(1) Forcing or requiring any employer or self-employed person to join any labor or employer organization or to enter into any agreement which is prohibited by Section 1154.5.

(2) Forcing or requiring any person to cease using, selling, transporting, or otherwise dealing in the products of any other producer, processor, or manufacturer, or to cease doing business with any other person, or forcing or requiring any other employer to recognize or bargain with a labor organization as the representative

of his employees unless such labor organization has been certified as the representative of such employees. Nothing contained in this paragraph shall be construed to make unlawful, where not otherwise unlawful, any primary strike or primary picketing.

(3) Forcing or requiring any employer to recognize or bargain with a particular labor organization as the representative of his agricultural employees if another labor organization has been certified as the representative of such employees under the provisions of Chapter 5 (commencing with Section 1156) of this part.

(4) Forcing or requiring any employer to assign particular work to employees in a particular labor organization or in a particular trade, craft, or class, unless such employer is failing to conform to an order or certification of the board determining the bargaining representative for employees performing such work.

Nothing contained in this subdivision (d) shall be construed to prohibit publicity, including picketing for the purpose of truthfully advising the public, including consumers, that a product or products or ingredients thereof are produced by an agricultural employer with whom the labor organization has a primary dispute and are distributed by another employer, as long as such publicity does not have an effect of inducing any individual employed by any person other than the primary employer in the course of his employment to refuse to pick up, deliver, or transport any goods, or not to perform any services at the establishment of the employer engaged in such distribution, and as long as such publicity does not have the effect of requesting the public to cease patronizing such other employer.

However, publicity which includes picketing and has the effect of requesting the public to cease patronizing such other employer, shall be permitted only if the labor organization is currently certified as the representative of the primary employer's employees.

Further, publicity other than picketing, but including peaceful distribution of literature which has the effect of requesting the public to cease patronizing such other employer, shall be permitted only if the labor organization has not lost an election for the primary employer's employees within the preceding 12-month period, and no other labor organization is currently certified as the representative of the primary employer's employees.

Nothing contained in this subdivision (d) shall be construed to prohibit publicity, including picketing, which may not be prohibited under the United States Constitution or the California Constitution.

Nor shall anything in this subdivision (d) be construed to apply or be applicable to any labor organization in its representation of workers who are not agricultural employees. Any such labor organization shall continue to be governed in its intrastate activities for nonagricultural workers by Section 923 and applicable judicial precedents.

(e) To require of employees covered by an agreement authorized under subdivision (c) of Section 1153 the payment, as a condition precedent to becoming a member of such organization, of a fee in an amount which the board finds excessive or discriminatory under all circumstances. In making such a finding, the board shall consider, among other relevant factors, the practices and customs of labor organizations in the agriculture industry and the wages currently paid to the employees affected.

(f) To cause or attempt to cause an agricultural employer to pay or deliver, or agree to pay or deliver, any money or other thing of value, in the nature of an exaction, for services which are not performed or not to be performed.

(g) To picket or cause to be picketed, or threaten to picket or cause to be picketed, any employer where an object thereof is either forcing or requiring an employer to recognize or bargain with a labor organization as the representative of his employees, or forcing or requiring the employees of an employer to accept or select such labor organization as their collective-bargai ning representative, unless such labor organization is currently certified as the representative of such employees, in any of the following cases:

(1) Where the employer has lawfully recognized in accordance with this part any other labor organization and a question concerning representation may not appropriately be raised under Section 1156.3.

(2) Where within the preceding 12 months a valid election under Chapter 5 (commencing with Section 1156) of this part has been conducted.

Nothing in this subdivision shall be construed to prohibit any picketing or other publicity for the purpose of truthfully advising the public (including consumers) that an employer does not employ members of, or have a contract with, a labor organization, unless an effect of such picketing is to induce any individual employed by any other person in the course of his employment, not to pick up, deliver, or transport any goods or not to perform any services.

Nothing in this subdivision (g) shall be construed to permit any act which would otherwise be an unfair labor practice under this section.

(h) To picket or cause to be picketed, or threaten to picket or cause to be picketed, any employer where an object thereof is either forcing or requiring an employer to recognize or bargain with the labor organization as a representative of his employees unless such labor organization is currently certified as the collective-bargaining representative of such employees.

(i) Nothing contained in this section shall be construed to make unlawful a refusal by any person to enter upon the premises of any agricultural employer, other than his own employer, if the employees of such employer are engaged in a strike ratified or approved by a representative of such employees whom such employer is required to recognize under this part.

1154.5. It shall be an unfair labor practice for any labor organization which represents the employees of the employer and such employer to enter into any contract or agreement, express or implied, whereby such employer ceases or refrains, or agrees to cease or refrain, from handling, using, selling, transporting, or otherwise dealing in any of the products of any other employer, or to cease doing business with any other person, and any contract or agreement entered into heretofore or hereafter containing such an agreement shall be, to such extent, unenforceable and void. Nothing in this section shall apply to an agreement between a labor organization and an employer relating to a supplier of an ingredient or ingredients which are integrated into a product produced or distributed by such employer where the labor organization is certified as the representative of the employees of such supplier, but no collective-bargaining agreement between such supplier and such labor organization is in effect. Further, nothing in this section shall apply to an agreement between a labor organization and an agricultural employer relating to the contracting or subcontracting of work to be done at the site of the farm and related operations. Nothing in this part shall prohibit the enforcement of any agreement which is within the foregoing exceptions.

Nor shall anything in this section be construed to apply or be applicable to any labor organization in its representation of workers who are not agricultural employees. Any such labor organization shall continue to be governed in its intrastate activities for nonagricultural workers by Section 923 and applicable judicial precedents.

1154.6. It shall be an unfair labor practice for an employer or labor organization, or their agents, willfully to arrange for persons to become employees for the primary purpose of voting in elections.

1155. The expressing of any views, arguments, or opinions, or the dissemination thereof, whether in written, printed, graphic, or visual form, shall not constitute evidence of an unfair labor practice under the provisions of this part, if such expression contains no threat of reprisal or force, or promise of benefit.

1155.2. (a) For purposes of this part, to bargain collectively in good faith is the performance of the mutual obligation of the agricultural employer and the representative of the agricultural employees to meet at reasonable times and confer in good faith with respect to wages, hours, and other terms and conditions of employment, or the negotiation of an agreement, or any questions arising thereunder, and the execution of a written contract incorporating any agreement reached if requested by either party, but such obligation does not compel either party to agree to a proposal or require the making of a concession.

(b) Upon the filing by any person of a petition not earlier than the 90th day nor later than the 60th day preceding the expiration of the 12-month period following initial certification, the board shall determine whether an employer has bargained in good faith with the currently certified labor organization. If the board finds that the employer has not bargained in good faith, it may extend the certification for up to one additional year, effective immediately upon the expiration of the previous 12-month period following initial certification.

1155.3. (a) Where there is in effect a collective-bargaining contract covering agricultural employees, the duty to bargain collectively shall also mean that no party to such contract shall terminate or modify such contract, unless the party desiring such termination or modification does all of the following:

(1) Serves a written notice upon the other party to the contract of the proposed termination or modification not less than 60 days prior to the expiration date thereof, or, in the event such contract contains no expiration date, 60 days prior to the time it is proposed to make such termination or modification.

(2) Offers to meet and confer with the other party for the purpose of negotiating a new contract or a contract containing the proposed modifications.

(3) Notifies the Conciliation Service of the State of California within 30 days after such notice of the existence of a dispute, provided no agreement has been reached by that time.

(4) Continues in full force and effect, without resorting to strike or lockout, all the terms and conditions of the existing contract, for a period of 60 days after such notice is given, or until the expiration date of such contract, whichever occurs later.

(b) The duties imposed upon agricultural employers and labor organizations by paragraphs (2), (3), and (4) of subdivision (a) shall become inapplicable upon an intervening certification of the board that the labor organization or individual which is a party to the contract has been superseded as, or has ceased to be the representative of the employees, subject to the provisions of Chapter 5 (commencing with Section 1156) of this part, and the duties so imposed shall not be construed to require either party to discuss or agree to any modification of the terms and conditions contained in a contract for a fixed period, if such modification is to become effective before such terms and conditions can be reopened under the provisions of the contract. Any agricultural employee who engages in a strike within the 60-day period specified in this section shall lose his status as an agricultural employee of the agricultural employer engaged in the particular labor dispute, for the purposes of Section 1153 to 1154 inclusive, and Chapters 5 (commencing with Section 1156) and 6 (commencing with Section 1160) of this part, but such loss of status for such employee shall terminate if and when he is reemployed by such employer.

1155.4. It shall be unlawful for any agricultural employer or association of agricultural employers, or any person who acts as a labor relations expert, adviser, or consultant to an agricultural employer, or who acts in the interest of an agricultural employer, to pay, lend, or deliver, any money or other thing of value to any of the following:

(a) Any representative of any of his agricultural employees.

(b) Any agricultural labor organization, or any officer or employee thereof, which represents, seeks to represent, or would admit to membership, any of the agricultural employees of such employer.

(c) Any employee or group or committee of employees of such employer in excess of their normal compensation for the purpose of causing such employee or group or committee directly or indirectly to influence any other employees in the exercise of the right to organize and bargain collectively through representatives of their own choosing.

(d) Any officer or employee of an agricultural labor organization with intent to influence him in respect to any of his actions, decisions, or duties as a representative of agricultural employees or as such officer or employee of such labor organization.

1155.5. It shall be unlawful for any person to request, demand, receive, or accept, or agree to receive or accept, any payment, loan, or delivery of any money or other thing of value prohibited by

Section 1155.4.

1155.6. Nothing in Section 1155.4 or 1155.5 shall apply to any matter set forth in subsection (c) of Section 186 of Title 29 of the United States Code.

1155.7. Nothing in this chapter shall be construed to apply or be applicable to any labor organization in its representation of workers who are not agricultural employees. Any such labor organization shall continue to be governed in its intrastate activities for nonagricultural workers by Section 923 and applicable judicial precedents.

1156. Representatives designated or selected by a secret ballot for the purposes of collective bargaining by the majority of the agricultural employees in the bargaining unit shall be the exclusive representatives of all the agricultural employees in such unit for the purpose of collective bargaining with respect to rates of pay, wages, hours of employment, or other conditions of employment. Any individual agricultural employee or a group of agricultural employees shall have the right at any time to present grievances to their agricultural employer and to have such grievances adjusted, without the intervention of the bargaining representative, as long as the adjustment is not inconsistent with the terms of a collective-bargaining contract or agreement then in effect, if the bargaining representative has been given opportunity to be present at such adjustment.

1156.2. The bargaining unit shall be all the agricultural employees of an employer. If the agricultural employees of the employer are employed in two or more noncontiguous geographical areas, the board shall determine the appropriate unit or units of agricultural employees in which a secret ballot election shall be conducted.

1156.3. (a) A petition that is either signed by, or accompanied by authorization cards signed by, a majority of the currently employed employees in the bargaining unit may be filed by an agricultural employee or group of agricultural employees, or any individual or labor organization acting on behalf of those agricultural employees, in accordance with any rules and regulations prescribed by the board. The petition shall allege all of the following:
(1) That the number of agricultural employees currently employed by the employer named in the petition, as determined from the employer's payroll immediately preceding the filing of the petition, is not less than 50 percent of the employer's peak agricultural employment for the current calendar year.
(2) That no valid election pursuant to this section has been conducted among the agricultural employees of the employer named in the petition within the 12 months immediately preceding the filing of the petition.
(3) That no labor organization is currently certified as the exclusive collective bargaining representative of the agricultural

employees of the employer named in the petition.

(4) That the petition is not barred by an existing collective bargaining agreement.

(b) Upon receipt of a signed petition, as described in subdivision (a), the board shall immediately investigate the petition. If the board has reasonable cause to believe that a bona fide question of representation exists, it shall direct a representation election by secret ballot to be held, upon due notice to all interested parties and within a maximum of seven days of the filing of the petition. If, at the time the election petition is filed, a majority of the employees in a bargaining unit are engaged in a strike, the board shall, with all due diligence, attempt to hold a secret ballot election within 48 hours of the filing of the petition. The holding of elections under strike circumstances shall take precedence over the holding of other secret ballot elections.

(c) The board shall make available at any election held under this chapter ballots printed in English and Spanish. The board may also make available at the election ballots printed in any other language as may be requested by an agricultural labor organization or any agricultural employee eligible to vote under this part. Every election ballot, except ballots in runoff elections where the choice is between labor organizations, shall provide the employee with the opportunity to vote against representation by a labor organization by providing an appropriate space designated "No Labor Organizations."

(d) Any other labor organization shall be qualified to appear on the ballot if it presents authorization cards signed by at least 20 percent of the employees in the bargaining unit at least 24 hours prior to the election.

(e) (1) Within five days after an election, any person may file with the board a signed petition asserting that allegations made in the petition filed pursuant to subdivision (a) were incorrect, asserting that the board improperly determined the geographical scope of the bargaining unit, or objecting to the conduct of the election or conduct affecting the results of the election.

(2) Upon receipt of a petition under this subdivision, the board, upon due notice, shall conduct a hearing to determine whether the election shall be certified. This hearing may be conducted by an officer or employee of a regional office of the board. The officer may not make any recommendations with respect to the certification of the election. The board may refuse to certify the election if it finds, on the record of the hearing, that any of the assertions made in the petition filed pursuant to this subdivision are correct, that the election was not conducted properly, or that misconduct affecting the results of the election occurred. The board shall certify the election unless it determines that there are sufficient grounds to refuse to do so.

(f) Notwithstanding any other provision of law, if the board refuses to certify an election because of employer misconduct that, in addition to affecting the results of the election, would render slight the chances of a new election reflecting the free and fair choice of employees, the labor organization shall be certified as the exclusive bargaining representative for the bargaining unit.

(g) If no petition is filed pursuant to subdivision (e) within five days of the election, the board shall certify the election.

(h) The board shall decertify a labor organization if either of the following occur:

(1) The Department of Fair Employment and Housing finds that the

labor organization engaged in discrimination on any basis listed in subdivision (a) of Section 12940 of the Government Code, as those bases are defined in Sections 12926 and 12926.1 of the Government Code, except as otherwise provided in Section 12940 of the Government Code.

(2) The United States Equal Employment Opportunity Commission finds, pursuant to Section 2000e-5 of Title 42 of the United States Code, that the labor organization engaged in discrimination on the basis of race, color, national origin, religion, sex, or any other arbitrary or invidious classification in violation of Subchapter VI of Chapter 21 of Title 42 of the United States Code during the period of the labor organization's present certification.

(i) (1) With regard to elections held pursuant to this section or Section 1156.7, the following time limits apply for action by the board, and agents acting pursuant to authority delegated by the board:

(A) (i) The board shall, within 21 days of the filing of election objections or the submittal of evidence in support of challenges to ballots, evaluate the election objections or challenged ballots and issue a decision determining which, if any, must be set for hearing.

(ii) The hearing on election objections or challenged ballots set pursuant to clause (i) shall be scheduled to commence within 28 days of the date of the board's decision to set a hearing.

(B) The investigative hearing examiner (IHE) appointed pursuant to Section 1145 shall issue a recommended decision within 60 days of the close of the hearing on the matters described in subparagraph (A). Upon mutual agreement of the parties, the IHE may extend the time period to issue a recommended decision by 30 days.

(C) The board shall issue a decision regarding the election objections or challenged ballots within 45 days of receipt of any exceptions to the decision of the IHE.

(2) The board may consolidate a challenged ballot hearing with a hearing on objections to an election.

(3) The board may grant extensions on the time limits specified in this subdivision upon a showing of good cause or by stipulation of all affected parties.

1156.4. Recognizing that agriculture is a seasonal occupation for a majority of agricultural employees, and wishing to provide the fullest scope for employees' enjoyment of the rights included in this part, the board shall not consider a representation petition or a petition to decertify as timely filed unless the employer's payroll reflects 50 percent of the peak agricultural employment for such employer for the current calendar year for the payroll period immediately preceding the filing of the petition.

In this connection, the peak agricultural employment for the prior season shall alone not be a basis for such determination, but rather the board shall estimate peak employment on the basis of acreage and crop statistics which shall be applied uniformly throughout the State of California and upon all other relevant data.

1156.5. The board shall not direct an election in any bargaining unit where a valid election has been held in the immediately preceding 12-month period.

1156.6.   The board shall not direct an election in any bargaining unit which is represented by a labor organization that has been certified within the immediately preceding 12-month period or whose certification has been extended pursuant to subdivision (b) of Section 1155.2.

1156.7.   (a) No collective-bargaining agreement executed prior to the effective date of this chapter shall bar a petition for an election.

(b) A collective-bargaining agreement executed by an employer and a labor organization certified as the exclusive bargaining representative of his employees pursuant to this chapter shall be a bar to a petition for an election among such employees for the term of the agreement, but in any event such bar shall not exceed three years, provided that both the following conditions are met:

(1) The agreement is in writing and executed by all parties thereto.

(2) It incorporates the substantive terms and conditions of employment of such employees.

(c) Upon the filing with the board by an employee or group of employees of a petition signed by 30 percent or more of the agricultural employees in a bargaining unit represented by a certified labor organization which is a party to a valid collective-bargaining agreement, requesting that such labor organization be decertified, the board shall conduct an election by secret ballot pursuant to the applicable provisions of this chapter, and shall certify the results to such labor organization and employer.

However, such a petition shall not be deemed timely unless it is filed during the year preceding the expiration of a collective-bargaining agreement which would otherwise bar the holding of an election, and when the number of agricultural employees is not less than 50 percent of the employer's peak agricultural employment for the current calendar year.

(d) Upon the filing with the board of a signed petition by an agricultural employee or group of agricultural employees, or any individual or labor organization acting in their behalf, accompanied by authorization cards signed by a majority of the employees in an appropriate bargaining unit, and alleging all the conditions of paragraphs (1), (2), and (3), the board shall immediately investigate such petition and, if it has reasonable cause to believe that a bona fide question of representation exists, it shall direct an election by secret ballot pursuant to the applicable provisions of this chapter:

(1) That the number of agricultural employees currently employed by the employer named in the petition, as determined from his payroll immediately preceding the filing of the petition, is not less than 50 percent of his peak agricultural employment for the current calendar year.

(2) That no valid election pursuant to this section has been conducted among the agricultural employees of the employer named in the petition within the 12 months immediately preceding the filing thereof.

(3) That a labor organization, certified for an appropriate unit, has a collective-bargaining agreement with the employer which would

otherwise bar the holding of an election and that this agreement will expire within the next 12 months.

1157. All agricultural employees of the employer whose names appear on the payroll applicable to the payroll period immediately preceding the filing of the petition of such an election shall be eligible to vote. An economic striker shall be eligible to vote under such regulations as the board shall find are consistent with the purposes and provisions of this part in any election, provided that the striker who has been permanently replaced shall not be eligible to vote in any election conducted more than 12 months after the commencement of the strike.

In the case of elections conducted within 18 months of the effective date of this part which involve labor disputes which commenced prior to such effective date, the board shall have the jurisdiction to adopt fair, equitable, and appropriate eligibility rules, which shall effectuate the policies of this part, with respect to the eligibility of economic strikers who were paid for work performed or for paid vacation during the payroll period immediately preceding the expiration of a collective-bargaining agreement or the commencement of a strike; provided, however, that in no event shall the board afford eligibility to any such striker who has not performed any services for the employer during the 36-month period immediately preceding the effective date of this part.

1157.2. In any election where none of the choices on the ballot receives a majority, a runoff shall be conducted, the ballot providing for a selection between the two choices receiving the largest and second largest number of valid votes cast in the election.

1157.3. Employers shall maintain accurate and current payroll lists containing the names and addresses of all their employees, and shall make such lists available to the board upon request.

1158. Whenever an order of the board made pursuant to Section 1160.3 is based in whole or in part upon the facts certified following an investigation pursuant to Sections 1156.3 to 1157.2, inclusive, and there is a petition for review of the order, the certification and the record of the investigation shall be included in the transcript of the entire record required to be filed under Section 1160.8 and thereupon the decree of the court enforcing, modifying, or setting aside in whole or in part the order of the board shall be made and entered upon the pleadings, testimony, and proceedings set forth in the transcript. The filing of a petition for review described in this section shall not be grounds for a stay of proceedings conducted pursuant to Chapter 6.5 (commencing with Section 1164).

1159. In order to assure the full freedom of association, self-organization, and designation of representatives of the employees own choosing, only labor organizations certified pursuant

to this part shall be parties to a legally valid
collective-bargaining agreement.

1160.   The board is empowered, as provided in this chapter, to
prevent any person from engaging in any unfair labor practice, as set
forth in Chapter 4 (commencing with Section 1153) of this part.

1160.2.   Whenever it is charged that any person has engaged in or is
engaging in any such unfair labor practice, the board, or any agent
or agency designated by the board for such purposes, shall have power
to issue and cause to be served upon such person a complaint stating
the charges in that respect, and containing a notice of hearing
before the board or a member thereof, or before a designated agency
or agencies, at a place therein fixed, not less than five days after
the serving of such complaint. No complaint shall issue based upon
any unfair labor practice occurring more than six months prior to the
filing of the charge with the board and the service of a copy
thereof upon the person against whom such charge is made, unless the
person aggrieved thereby was prevented from filing such charge by
reason of service in the armed forces, in which event the six-month
period shall be computed from the day of his discharge. Any such
complaint may be amended by the member, agent, or agency conducting
the hearing, or the board in its discretion, at any time prior to the
issuance of an order based thereon. The person so complained
against shall have the right to file an answer to the original or
amended complaint and to appear in person or otherwise and give
testimony at the place and time fixed in the complaint. In the
discretion of the member, agent, or agency conducting the hearing or
the board, any other person may be allowed to intervene in the
proceeding and to present testimony. Any such proceeding shall, so
far as practicable, be conducted in accordance with the Evidence
Code. All proceedings shall be appropriately reported.

1160.3.   The testimony taken by such member, agent, or agency, or
the board in such hearing shall be reduced to writing and filed with
the board. Thereafter, in its discretion, the board, upon notice,
may take further testimony or hear argument. If, upon the
preponderance of the testimony taken, the board shall be of the
opinion that any person named in the complaint has engaged in or is
engaging in any such unfair labor practice, the board shall state its
findings of fact and shall issue and cause to be served on such
person an order requiring such person to cease and desist from such
unfair labor practice, to take affirmative action, including
reinstatement of employees with or without backpay, and making
employees whole, when the board deems such relief appropriate, for
the loss of pay resulting from the employer's refusal to bargain, and
to provide such other relief as will effectuate the policies of this
part. Where an order directs reinstatement of an employee, backpay
may be required of the employer or labor organization, as the case
may be, responsible for the discrimination suffered by him. Such
order may further require such person to make reports from time to
time showing the extent to which it has complied with the order. If,
upon the preponderance of the testimony taken, the board shall be of

the opinion that the person named in the complaint has not engaged
in or is not engaging in any unfair labor practice, the board shall
state its findings of fact and shall issue an order dismissing the
complaint. No order of the board shall require the reinstatement of
any individual as an employee who has been suspended or discharged,
or the payment to him of any backpay, if such individual was
suspended or discharged for cause. In case the evidence is presented
before a member of the board, or before an administrative law
officer thereof, such member, or such administrative law officer, as
the case may be, shall issue and cause to be served on the parties to
the proceedings a proposed report, together with a recommended
order, which shall be filed with the board, and, if no exceptions are
filed within 20 days after service thereof upon such parties, or
within such further period as the board may authorize, such
recommended order shall become the order of the board and become
effective as therein prescribed.

Until the record in a case shall have been filed in a court, as
provided in this chapter, the board may, at any time upon reasonable
notice and in such manner as it shall deem proper, modify or set
aside, in whole or in part, any finding or order made or issued by
it.

1160.4. (a) The board may, upon finding reasonable cause to believe
that any person has engaged in or is engaging in an unfair labor
practice, petition the superior court in any county wherein the
unfair labor practice in question is alleged to have occurred, or
wherein the person resides or transacts business, for appropriate
temporary relief or restraining order. Upon the filing of the
petition, the board shall cause notice thereof to be served upon the
person, and thereupon the court shall have jurisdiction to grant to
the board such temporary relief or restraining order as the court
deems just and proper.

(b) (1) In addition to any harm resulting directly from an adverse
employment action or other allegedly unlawful action, the court
shall consider the indirect effect upon protected rights of all
agricultural employees of the employer in determining whether
temporary relief or a restraining order is just and proper.

(2) When the alleged unfair labor practice is such that, by its
nature, it would interfere with the free choice of employees to
choose or not choose an exclusive bargaining representative,
appropriate temporary relief or a restraining order shall issue on a
showing that reasonable cause exists to believe that the unfair labor
practice has occurred. The order shall remain in effect until an
election has been held or for 30 days, whichever occurs first.
Thereafter, a preliminary injunction may issue if it is shown to be
just and proper.

(c) Notwithstanding Section 916 of the Code of Civil Procedure,
temporary relief or restraining orders granted pursuant to this
section shall not be stayed pending appeal.

1160.5. Whenever it is charged that any person has engaged in an
unfair labor practice within the meaning of paragraph (4) of
subdivision (d) of Section 1154, the board is empowered and directed
to hear and determine the dispute out of which such unfair labor
practice shall have arisen, unless within 10 days after notice that

such charge has been filed, the parties to such dispute submit to the board satisfactory evidence that they have adjusted, or agreed upon methods for the voluntary adjustment of the dispute. Upon compliance by the parties to the dispute with the decision of the board or upon such voluntary adjustment of the dispute, such charge shall be dismissed.

1160.6. Whenever it is charged that any person has engaged in an unfair labor practice within the meaning of paragraph (1), (2), or (3) of subdivision (d), or of subdivision (g), of Section 1154, or of Section 1155, the preliminary investigation of such charge shall be made forthwith and given priority over all other cases except cases of like character in the office where it is filed or to which it is referred. If, after such investigation, the officer or regional attorney to whom the matter may be referred has reasonable cause to believe such charge is true and that a complaint should issue, he shall, on behalf of the board, petition the superior court in the county in which the unfair labor practice in question has occurred, is alleged to have occurred, or where the person alleged to have committed the unfair labor practice resides or transacts business, for appropriate injunctive relief pending the final adjudication of the board with respect to the matter. The officer or regional attorney shall make all reasonable efforts to advise the party against whom the restraining order is sought of his intention to seek such order at least 24 hours prior to doing so. In the event the officer or regional attorney has been unable to advise such party of his intent at least 24 hours in advance, he shall submit a declaration to the court under penalty of perjury setting forth in detail the efforts he has made. Upon the filing of any such petition, the superior court shall have jurisdiction to grant such injunctive relief or temporary restraining order as it deems just and proper. Upon the filing of any such petition, the board shall cause notice thereof to be served upon any person involved in the charge and such person, including the charging party, shall be given an opportunity to appear by counsel and present any relevant testimony. For the purposes of this section, the superior court shall be deemed to have jurisdiction of a labor organization either in the county in which such organization maintains its principal office, or in any county in which its duly authorized officers or agents are engaged in promoting or protecting the interests of employee members. The service of legal process upon such officer or agent shall constitute service upon the labor organization and make such organization a party to the suit. In situations where such relief is appropriate, the procedure specified herein shall apply to charges with respect to paragraph (4) of subdivision (d) of Section 1154.

1160.7. Whenever it is charged that any person has engaged in an unfair labor practice within the meaning of subdivision (c) of Section 1153 or subdivision (b) of Section 1154, such charge shall be given priority over all other cases except cases of like character in the office where it is filed or to which it is referred and cases given priority under Section 1160.6.

1160.8. Any person aggrieved by the final order of the board granting or denying in whole or in part the relief sought may obtain a review of such order in the court of appeal having jurisdiction over the county wherein the unfair labor practice in question was alleged to have been engaged in, or wherein such person resides or transacts business, by filing in such court a written petition requesting that the order of the board be modified or set aside. Such petition shall be filed with the court within 30 days from the date of the issuance of the board's order. Upon the filing of such petition, the court shall cause notice to be served upon the board and thereupon shall have jurisdiction of the proceeding. The board shall file in the court the record of the proceeding, certified by the board within 10 days after the clerk's notice unless such time is extended by the court for good cause shown. The court shall have jurisdiction to grant to the board such temporary relief or restraining order it deems just and proper and in like manner to make and enter a decree enforcing, modifying and enforcing as so modified, or setting aside in whole or in part, the order of the board. The findings of the board with respect to questions of fact if supported by substantial evidence on the record considered as a whole shall in like manner be conclusive.

An order directing an election shall not be stayed pending review, but such order may be reviewed as provided in Section 1158.

If the time for review of the board order has lapsed, and the person has not voluntarily complied with the board's order, the board may apply to the superior court in any county in which the unfair labor practice occurred or wherein such person resides or transacts business for enforcement of its order. If after hearing, the court determines that the order was issued pursuant to procedures established by the board and that the person refuses to comply with the order, the court shall enforce such order by writ of injunction or other proper process. The court shall not review the merits of the order.

1160.9. The procedures set forth in this chapter shall be the exclusive method of redressing unfair labor practices.

1161. (a) The Agricultural Employee Relief Fund is hereby created as a special fund in the State Treasury and is continuously appropriated to the Agricultural Labor Relations Board for the purposes specified in subdivision (c). The board shall act as a trustee of all moneys deposited in the fund.

(b) Any monetary relief ordered by the board pursuant to this part to be paid by an employer to an employee shall be collected by the board on behalf of the employee. All monetary relief so collected by the board shall be remitted to the employee for whom the board collected the money.

(c) (1) Notwithstanding Section 1519 of the Code of Civil Procedure, if the board has made a diligent effort to locate an employee on whose behalf the board has collected monetary relief pursuant to this part, and is unable to locate the employee or the lawful representative of the employee for a period of two years after the date the board collected the monetary relief, the board shall deposit those moneys in the fund.

(2) Moneys in the fund shall be used by the board to pay employees

the unpaid balance of any monetary relief ordered by the board to be paid by an employer to an employee. Prior to making any payment from the fund, the board first shall make a finding that, in an individual case, the collection of the full amount of the monetary relief ordered is not possible after reasonable efforts have been made to collect the balance from the employer.

(d) As used in this section, "fund" means the Agricultural Employee Relief Fund.

(e) On or before July 1, 2002, the board shall report to the Legislature on the status of the fund.

1164. (a) An agricultural employer or a labor organization certified as the exclusive bargaining agent of a bargaining unit of agricultural employees may file with the board, at any time following (1) 90 days after a renewed demand to bargain by an agricultural employer or a labor organization certified prior to January 1, 2003, which meets the conditions specified in Section 1164.11, (2) 90 days after an initial request to bargain by an agricultural employer or a labor organization certified after January 1, 2003, (3) 60 days after the board has certified the labor organization pursuant to subdivision (f) of Section 1156.3, or (4) 60 days after the board has dismissed a decertification petition upon a finding that the employer has unlawfully initiated, supported, sponsored, or assisted in the filing of a decertification petition a declaration that the parties have failed to reach a collective bargaining agreement and a request that the board issue an order directing the parties to mandatory mediation and conciliation of their issues. "Agricultural employer," for purposes of this chapter, means an agricultural employer, as defined in subdivision (c) of Section 1140.4, who has employed or engaged 25 or more agricultural employees during any calendar week in the year preceding the filing of a declaration pursuant to this subdivision.

(b) Upon receipt of a declaration pursuant to subdivision (a), the board shall immediately issue an order directing the parties to mandatory mediation and conciliation of their issues. The board shall request from the California State Mediation and Conciliation Service a list of nine mediators who have experience in labor mediation. The California State Mediation and Conciliation Service may include names chosen from its own mediators, or from a list of names supplied by the American Arbitration Association or the Federal Mediation Service. The parties shall select a mediator from the list within seven days of receipt of the list. If the parties cannot agree on a mediator, they shall strike names from the list until a mediator is chosen by process of elimination. If a party refuses to participate in selecting a mediator, the other party may choose a mediator from the list. The costs of mediation and conciliation shall be borne equally by the parties.

(c) Upon appointment, the mediator shall immediately schedule meetings at a time and location reasonably accessible to the parties. Mediation shall proceed for a period of 30 days. Upon expiration of the 30-day period, if the parties do not resolve the issues to their mutual satisfaction, the mediator shall certify that the mediation process has been exhausted. Upon mutual agreement of the parties, the mediator may extend the mediation period for an additional 30 days.

(d) Within 21 days, the mediator shall file a report with the board that resolves all of the issues between the parties and establishes the final terms of a collective bargaining agreement, including all issues subject to mediation and all issues resolved by the parties prior to the certification of the exhaustion of the mediation process. With respect to any issues in dispute between the parties, the report shall include the basis for the mediator's determination. The mediator's determination shall be supported by the record.

(e) In resolving the issues in dispute, the mediator may consider those factors commonly considered in similar proceedings, including:

(1) The stipulations of the parties.

(2) The financial condition of the employer and its ability to meet the costs of the contract in those instances where the employer claims an inability to meet the union's wage and benefit demands.

(3) The corresponding wages, benefits, and terms and conditions of employment in other collective bargaining agreements covering similar agricultural operations with similar labor requirements.

(4) The corresponding wages, benefits, and terms and conditions of employment prevailing in comparable firms or industries in geographical areas with similar economic conditions, taking into account the size of the employer, the skills, experience, and training required of the employees, and the difficulty and nature of the work performed.

(5) The average consumer prices for goods and services according to the California Consumer Price Index, and the overall cost of living, in the area where the work is performed.

1164.3. (a) Either party, within seven days of the filing of the report by the mediator, may petition the board for review of the report. The petitioning party shall, in the petition, specify the particular provisions of the mediator's report for which it is seeking review by the board and shall specify the specific grounds authorizing review by the board. The board, within 10 days of receipt of a petition, may accept for review those portions of the petition for which a prima facie case has been established that (1) a provision of the collective bargaining agreement set forth in the mediator's report is unrelated to wages, hours, or other conditions of employment within the meaning of Section 1155.2, (2) a provision of the collective bargaining agreement set forth in the mediator's report is based on clearly erroneous findings of material fact, or (3) a provision of the collective bargaining agreement set forth in the mediator's report is arbitrary or capricious in light of the mediator's findings of fact.

(b) If it finds grounds exist to grant review within the meaning of subdivision (a), the board shall order the provisions of the report that are not the subject of the petition for review into effect as a final order of the board. If the board does not accept a petition for review or no petition for review is filed, then the mediator's report shall become a final order of the board.

(c) The board shall issue a decision concerning the petition and if it determines that a provision of the collective bargaining agreement contained in the mediator's report violates the provisions of subdivision (a), it shall, within 21 days, issue an order requiring the mediator to modify the terms of the collective bargaining agreement. The mediator shall meet with the parties for additional mediation for a period not to exceed 30 days. At the expiration of this mediation period, the mediator shall prepare a second report resolving any outstanding issues. The second report shall be filed with the board.

(d) Either party, within seven days of the filing of the mediator's second report, may petition the board for a review of the mediator's second report pursuant to the procedures specified in subdivision (a). If no petition is filed, the mediator's report shall take immediate effect as a final order of the board. If a petition is filed, the board shall issue an order confirming the mediator's report and order it into immediate effect, unless it finds that the report is subject to review for any of the grounds specified in subdivision (a), in which case the board shall determine the issues and shall issue a final order of the board.

(e) Either party, within seven days of the filing of the report by the mediator, may petition the board to set aside the report if a prima facie case is established that any of the following have occurred: (1) the mediator's report was procured by corruption, fraud, or other undue means, (2) there was corruption in the mediator, or (3) the rights of the petitioning party were substantially prejudiced by the misconduct of the mediator. For the sole purpose of interpreting the terms of paragraphs (1), (2), and (3), case law that interprets similar terms used in Section 1286.2 of the Code of Civil Procedure shall apply. If the board finds that any of these grounds exist, the board shall within 10 days vacate the report of the mediator and shall order the selection and appointment of a new mediator, and an additional mediation period of 30 days, pursuant to Section 1164.

(f) Within 60 days after the order of the board takes effect, either party or the board may file an action to enforce the order of the board, in the superior court for the County of Sacramento or in the county where either party's principal place of business is located. No final order of the board shall be stayed during any appeal under this section, unless the court finds that (1) the appellant will be irreparably harmed by the implementation of the board's order, and (2) the appellant has demonstrated a likelihood of success on appeal.

1164.5. (a) Within 30 days after the order of the board takes effect, a party may petition for a writ of review in the court of appeal or the California Supreme Court. If the writ issues, it shall be made returnable at a time and place specified by court order and shall direct the board to certify its record in the case to the court within the time specified. The petition for review shall be served personally upon the executive director of the board and the nonappealing party personally or by service.

(b) The review by the court shall not extend further than to determine, on the basis of the entire record, whether any of the following occurred:

(1) The board acted without, or in excess of, its powers or jurisdiction.

(2) The board has not proceeded in the manner required by law.

(3) The order or decision of the board was procured by fraud or was an abuse of discretion.

(4) The order or decision of the board violates any right of the petitioner under the Constitution of the United States or the California Constitution.

(c) Nothing in this section shall be construed to permit the court to hold a trial de novo, to take evidence other than as specified by the California Rules of Court, or to exercise its independent judgment on the evidence.

1164.7. (a) The board and each party to the action or proceeding before the mediator may appear in the review proceeding. Upon the hearing, the court of appeal or the Supreme Court shall enter judgment either affirming or setting aside the order of the board.
   (b) The provisions of the Code of Civil Procedure relating to writs of review shall, so far as applicable, apply to proceedings instituted under this chapter.

1164.9. No court of this state, except the court of appeal or the Supreme Court, to the extent specified in this article, shall have jurisdiction to review, reverse, correct, or annul any order or decision of the board to suspend or delay the execution or operation thereof, or to enjoin, restrain, or interfere with the board in the performance of its official duties, as provided by law and the rules of court.

1164.11. A demand made pursuant to paragraph (1) of subdivision (a) of Section 1164 may be made only in cases which meet all of the following criteria: (a) the parties have failed to reach agreement for at least one year after the date on which the labor organization made its initial request to bargain, (b) the employer has committed an unfair labor practice, and (c) the parties have not previously had a binding contract between them.

1164.12. To ensure an orderly implementation of the mediation process ordered by this chapter, a party may not file a total of more than 75 declarations with the board prior to January 1, 2008. In calculating the number of declarations so filed, the identity of the other party with respect to whom the declaration is filed, shall be irrelevant.

1164.13. The provisions of this chapter are severable. If any provision of this chapter or its application is held invalid, that invalidity shall not affect other provisions or applications that can be given effect without the invalid provision or application.

1165. (a) Suits for violation of contracts between an agricultural employer and an agricultural labor organization representing agricultural employees, as defined in this part, or between any such labor organizations, may be brought in any superior court having jurisdiction of the parties, without respect to the amount in controversy.
   (b) Any agricultural labor organization which represents agricultural employees and any agricultural employer shall be bound by the acts of its agents. Any such labor organization may sue or be

sued as an entity and in behalf of the employees whom it represents in the courts of this state. Any money judgment against a labor organization in a superior court shall be enforceable only against the organization as an entity and against its assets, and shall not be enforceable against any individual member or his assets.

1165.2.   For the purpose of this part, the superior court shall have jurisdiction over a labor organization in this state if such organization maintains its principal office in this state, or if its duly authorized officers or agents are engaged in representing or acting for employee members.

1165.3.   The service of summons, subpoena, or other legal process of any superior court upon an officer or agent of a labor organization, in his capacity as such, shall constitute service upon the labor organization.

1165.4.   For the purpose of this part, in determining whether any person is acting as an agent of another person so as to make such other person responsible for his acts, the question of whether the specific acts performed were actually authorized or subsequently ratified shall not be controlling.

1166.   Nothing in this part, except as specifically provided for herein, shall be construed so as either to interfere with or impede or diminish in any way the right to strike, or to affect the limitations or qualifications on such right.

1166.2.   Nothing in this part shall prohibit any individual employed as a supervisor from becoming or remaining a member of a labor organization, but no employer subject to this part shall be compelled to deem individuals defined herein as supervisors as employees for the purpose of any law, either national or local, relating to collective bargaining.

1166.3.   (a) If any provision of this part, or the application of such provision to any person or circumstances, shall be held invalid, the remainder of this part, or the application of such provision to persons or circumstances other than those as to which it is held invalid, shall not be affected thereby.
   (b) If any other act of the Legislature shall conflict with the provisions of this part, this part shall prevail.